ISBN: 9781983340420

A Picture Book

A WADDL & Little Green Pea Publication 2nd Edition 2020

Photography, content and design by Anna Carey, all quotes by Lydia Carey.

Other publications and more information available at www.littlegreenpea.co.uk

little green pea

For my beautiful brave super-girls who have been courageous enough to put this together for other families just like ours.

Anna Carey

A stranger called Mummy

what I think about adoption

By Lydia, Age 6

I love bedtime stories, cuddles and most of all
sandwiches

and I want to help other children who are like
me...

I am Lydia age 6

(and some quarters)

Dear Little Person,

(or big person)

One.

Welcome to your
new Family

The most
important
thing
is...

they really
do want to

Love

you.

tw⬡.

Stretch your legs out,
and take a BIG breath
and be brave.

three.

If you tell a grown up
they might help you.

It's like...

if you really want to do colouring,
but you don't know how to ask,
so you say;

"Mummy or Daddy,

please can I do

colouring

...PLEASE?"

and then

they do actually let you!

four.

Social Workers are actually good.

It's their job to see
if your family
is safe
that's why
sometimes
they have
to
move you
...like me.

five.

It takes a lot of time
to know things.

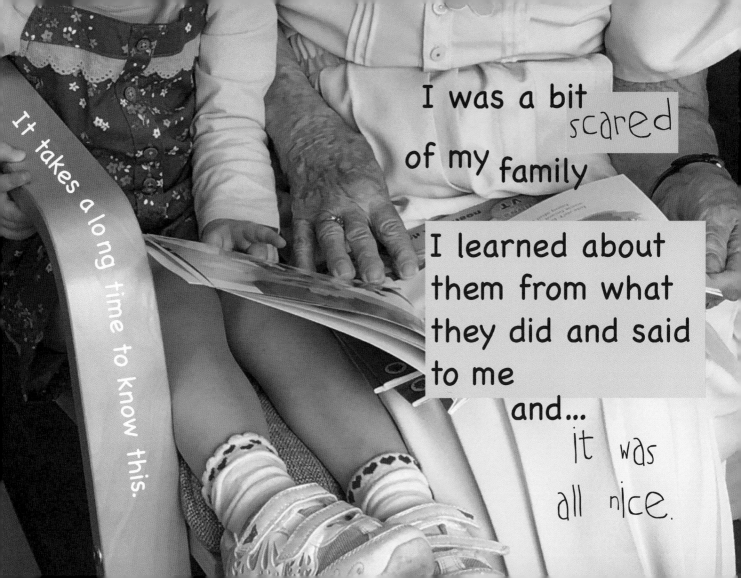

six.

They are your family
for...ever!

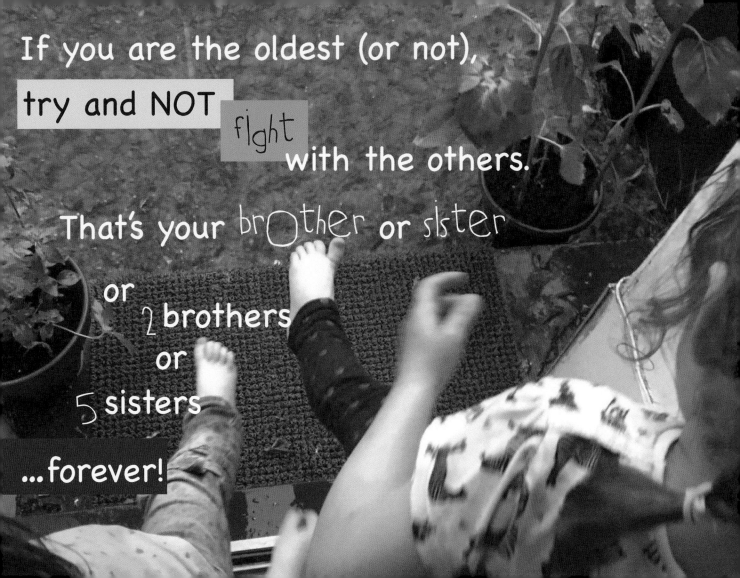

If you are the oldest (or not), try and NOT fight with the others.

That's your brother or sister

or 2 brothers or 5 sisters

...forever!

seven.

school and friends stuff is all
okay once you try it.

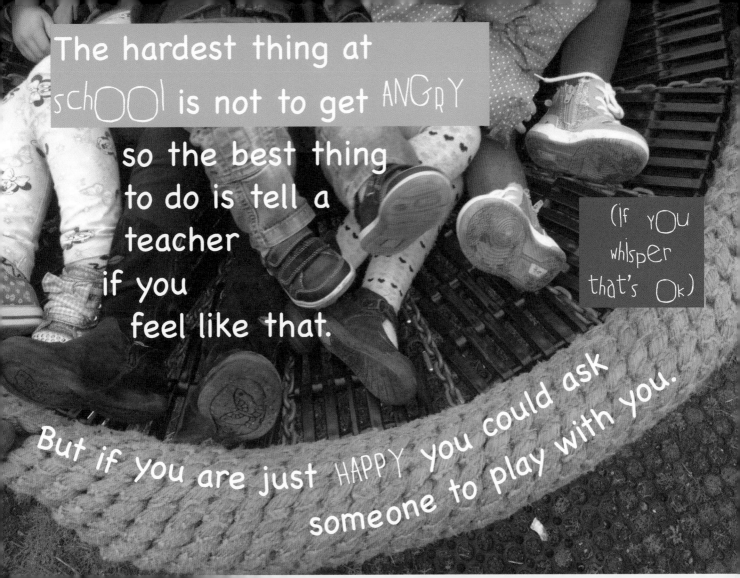

The hardest thing at schOOl is not to get ANGRY

so the best thing to do is tell a teacher if you feel like that.

(If you whisper that's Ok)

But if you are just HAPPY you could ask someone to play with you.

eight.

You might want
to say Thank you.

You might not have many tOys and your new family will buy you some.

You might want to say "Thank yOu" or cuddle them.

nine.

Remember
yOu will be all right
at the end.

If bad things happened like with me...

Mummy and Daddy will tell you how to talk more

and

look after you

They definitely look after you.

They help you learn

ten.

Be HAPPY if you can.

and next...

Dear Teachers,

When we first come you need to help us
a bit more because we might not know
what to do,

or

we might be scared.

Dear Friends and Family

If we say 'please can we have the same plate?' then you're making us upset if you don't let us have it.

Changing lots of things makes my tummy have the same feelings like when my family changed.

Dear Grandparents:

When you don't know who your Grandma is going to be, it really might be scary. It makes you think..

what if she is nasty? Then what would I do?

(We don't know Social Workers have even checked if you are going to be kind)

Dear new Mummy

If we do be naughty, can you tell us
off still, but gently, because we
might cry a lot, because we are
scared of you...
because you are really a
stranger called MUMMY.

littlegreenpea.co.uk

Printed in Great Britain
by Amazon